Sam Ll   ts. He
has wri   ens of novels set on the
sea,   ren's

DATE DUE

			PRINTED IN U.S.A.

EUROPE,
1805

Admiral
NELSON

WHO WAS...

Admiral
NELSON

*The sailor who
dared all
to win*

SAM LLEWELLYN

✳ SHORT BOOKS

First published in 2004 by
Short Books
15 Highbury Terrace
London N5 1UP

10 9 8 7 6 5 4 3 2 1

A CIP catalogue record for this book
is available from the British Library.

ISBN 1-904095-65-8

Printed in Great Britain by
Bookmarque Ltd, Croydon, Surrey

1805

The British fleet at sea. The ships white towers of canvas in line, exactly spaced one behind the other, nodding as the great blue waves roll under. At the front of the line, HMS Victory *— a huge ship, built of English oak, her sides chequered black and yellow. A ship that is a floating, fighting town, sworn to wreck the enemies of His Majesty King George.*

There are officers, seamen, a surgeon, a parson, gun crews, small boys known as powder monkeys to bring ammunition to the guns, cooks, carpenters, a black-smith, sailmakers to make the sails and topmen to set them, servants, boats' crews, sea-going soldiers called marines in lobster-red coats and white cross-straps, a parrot, pigs, a goat, the ship's cat with her new kittens. The Victory's decks, this dawn as every dawn, scrubbed white with holystones, flogged dry with ropes. She is a gleaming thing, neat, tidy, perfect. But not an ornament. Not an ornament at all.

Ships like the Victory were the biggest moving machines the world had ever seen. They travelled slowly but steadily, day after day, year after year, hardly pausing for food, never stopping to sleep, averaging perhaps a hundred miles a day...

Over the blue horizon ahead is Spain, Cape Trafalgar and the great port of Cadiz. The ships of France and Spain, allies in the war against England, are gathered in Cadiz harbour.

Between the Victory and Cadiz lie frigates – small, fast ships whose job is to keep their eyes open, and signal what they see to the fleet. The frigate's topmost mast is a whisker on the blue edge of the world. It carries signal flags. And the flags in this case say that the frigates have seen the enemy crews hauling their ships inch by inch closer to the harbour mouth.

Soon, joy of joys, the enemy will be out. And when they are out, they will have to fight. And when they fight, there will be a war lost or won.

A group of men stands on the quarterdeck at the back end of the Victory, *guarded by red marines. Men in dark blue coats with gold braid that flashes in the Spanish sun, swords at their sides, white breeches, shoes with silver buckles. The man at the centre of the group folds the telescope with which he has been looking at the frigate's signal. He is small, with a big nose in a thin face. Not an impressive man, at first sight.*

Actually, there is not much of him left. The right arm is gone, the empty sleeve pinned to the bosom of his coat under the stars of the decorations. The right eye is dull and filmy, quite blind. But the group looks down at this small person and listens intently to what he is saying.

The great battle is at hand. On the one side, Napoleon Bonaparte, Enemy of Liberty, Tyrant of the French. On the other, the one-armed, one-eyed man,

Admiral Lord Nelson of the Nile, Duke of Bronte, the Hero.

It has not always been like this.

Chapter 1

1771

The east wind blows cold off the river Medway at Chatham, on the Kent coast. It smells of mud and filth from the prison-ships anchored among the dirty-grey sandbanks. In March, it blows hard enough to knock your hat off. Particularly if you are young Horatio Nelson and the hat is a midshipman's hat, bought a couple of sizes too big, because you are only twelve years old and your father says you will grow into it. In the eighteenth century, midshipman was the most junior rank in the Royal Navy. Horatio Nelson planned to be in the Navy for the whole of his life.

Midshipman Horatio Nelson rescued his brand-new hat from the gutter, scrubbed off the worst of the tar and horse muck with the sleeve of his brand-new blue coat, and waited for someone to pay attention to him. The quay was crowded with men and boxes and barrels and piles of timber.

His sisters had packed him and his father into the coach in Norfolk. His father had accompanied him to London, and then put him into another coach to Chatham, where the *Raisonnable*, his uncle's ship, was lying. His father had looked sad, but Horatio had felt pretty big. He had felt medium-sized as the coach rattled south. And here on the quay, in this crowd of people with things to do, his uncle's ship a mere smudge in the darkening fog, he felt so small that it was no wonder he could not keep his hat on.

His father was a parson, his mother dead. The Rev. Nelson and his eight children lived crammed into a small house on the edge of the Norfolk marshes. Horatio Nelson had grown up among fishermen and the people who sailed cargo barges up the narrow creek to the quay at Burnham Overy Staithe. He helped them out, taking their mooring ropes, getting rides on the big, clumsy boats up the tide, trimming their baggy sails of thick tan canvas. They were soft-spoken people, happy to teach anyone who wanted to be taught.

But here on Chatham quay it was different. The men were hard and square, and when they talked they bellowed in voices loud enough to be heard above gales and cannon-fire. They moved fast and pitiless, never staying still long enough to be spoken to. It was out of the question that they would notice a parson's son, never big, who had for three days been shrinking steadily.

The hours passed. The night came down, wet and icy. The giant hat blew off again and again. Midshipman Horatio Nelson felt like weeping, but would not. He therefore summoned up the final remnants of his bigness. "Sir!" he cried to a vast man in a glazed round hat and bell-bottom trousers. "I am to be taken to the *Raisonnable*!"

"We got no orders," said the vast man, reeking of rum.

"If you please," said Nelson, "my uncle is the Captain."

"Captain's not on board," said the vast man.

"I am to be taken on board to wait for him," said Nelson. "I am so ordered."

Well, orders were orders. So all of a sudden, there was Horatio, standing by his new sea-chest in the stern of the big rowing-boat known as the cutter, holding his hat on his head, bound for the fog-shrouded *Raisonnable*, and a new life.

***

This was not at first very exciting. The *Raisonnable* was like a wet wooden cupboard. For a week or so he explored, feeling about the size of a mouse. Nobody paid him the slightest attention. Then one morning he heard the squeal of bosun's pipes, and caught sight of a figure huge and splendid in a gold-laced blue coat: his uncle, Maurice Suckling. Some time ago in Norfolk, Maurice Suckling had remarked that Horatio looked a bit puny for the Navy, and doubted that he would last long as a sailor. He would soon be proved wrong.

Big ships were not easy for small sailors. But on their decks they carried small boats, which they used to take men and weapons into water too shallow for their gigantic hulls. Nelson had been taught about small boats by his friends in Burnham, and so Uncle Maurice put him in command of one, with a crew of tough eggs. Horatio learned to thread the maze of sandbanks in the nearby Thames Estuary. It was cold, and wet, and difficult, but through constant practice he got good at it. Then his uncle sent him on a return trip to the West Indies on a merchant ship. By the time Horatio was fifteen, he had learned to be a seaman.

This was all very well. But being a seaman was not the same as being a sea officer. And to be a sea officer was Horatio Nelson's heart's desire.

***

1773

Just before his fifteenth birthday, Horatio heard that two chunky little ships called the *Carcass* and the *Racehorse* were being fitted out for an expedition to the North Pole. No boys were to be taken. This struck Nelson as deeply unfair. He sought out Captain Lutwidge, one of the expedition's commanders, and explained to him that, as a brilliant navigator of small boats, he would be valuable around the Pole. Like many others, Captain Lutwidge found that once this thin but ferocious midshipman had made up his mind, he would not take no for an answer.

The two ships set off up the west coast of Spitzbergen, an island only some 700 miles south of the Pole. Nelson (whose hat by now fitted him rather well) stood with his hands in his greatcoat pockets and the bitter wind at his back, watching the glittering icebergs slide by, imagining them transformed into trees, castles and monsters.

On they sailed north, until the sea froze and locked the ship in a mighty icefield. Watching from the deck, Nelson saw the huge, humpbacked shape of a polar bear slink behind a distant hillock of ice. Seizing muskets, he and a friend jumped onto the ice and ran towards the bear. The ship shrank behind them. A great silence fell, broken only by the split and boom of moving ice-floes.

"He's gone," said Nelson's friend.

At that moment the bear reared up, eight feet tall, spreading its gigantic fore-paws to grab and crush its attackers. Nelson put up his musket and pulled the trigger. Nothing happened; the powder was wet. Roaring, the bear advanced. Seizing the gun by the barrel, Nelson prepared to club the beast about the head.

At that moment there was an explosion from the ship, and a cannon-ball smashed a nearby ice-ridge to splinters. The bear hesitated, dropped on to all fours, and slunk away.

Captain Lutwidge was furious. "What do you mean

by rushing about hunting bears without telling a soul?" he roared.

Nelson was none too pleased himself. If Captain Lutwidge had not scared off the bear, he might have been able to beat it to death (it does not seem to have occurred to him that the bear might have won).

"Sir," he said, outraged. "I wished to kill a bear so that I might carry the skin to my father."

He then prepared his four-oared cutter, in which it looked as if he was going to have to seek help, the ships being frozen in. But at the last minute a change of wind broke up the ice, and the ships sailed south for England, home, and things more dangerous than bears.

***

Midshipmen became sea officers by passing the Lieutenant's examination. It seemed to Nelson that while he was good in small boats, across the Atlantic in a merchantman and in the Arctic, he had never served on a real fighting ship. So he made a fuss, and did not stop making a fuss until he had secured a berth on the *Seahorse*, a frigate of 20 guns, bound for the Indian Ocean. The *Seahorse* spent two years in the east, harassing the allies of Napoleon – including the unspeakable Indian ruler Hyder Ali, at whose navy Nelson fired his first shot in anger. Then, in a hot, mud-stinking creek off the Malabar coast, Nelson contracted a malarial fever.

It seemed probable that all the learning of sailing and navigation and signals had been a waste of effort. Such fevers used to kill off hundreds of men. Nelson lay sweating and freezing. In his delirium he cried for his poor dead mother. He cried because he had won the vast sum of £300 at cards, and he realised that he might have lost it instead, and been thrown out of the Navy, and landed in a debtor's prison, and disgraced his poor father. Round his bed the faces of the surgeons swam in and out of focus. He could tell they expected him to die.

But Nelson was never one to do what was expected.

***

1776

He recovered, a thin, yellow-eyed version of his former self. The surgeon in charge of him told him that unless he returned to England, he would die. So off he went, dragging himself through the sticky heat up the gangway of the frigate *Dolphin*, homeward bound. Once on board, he returned to bed and the grip of deep despair.

He had joined the Navy to achieve glory. And here he was, sick as a dog, tired out by the mere sound of the ship's company working on deck. He would never be an officer. His life was over.

One gloomy night, Nelson lay watching the moon-shadows of the windows on the deck, as colourless as his future. At that moment (he wrote later), he saw in his mind a pinpoint of brightness that swelled rapidly into a "Radiant Orb" that threw out light and warmth. With the light came happiness and confidence. "A sudden glow of patriotism was kindled within me, and presented my King and Country as my Patron."

He was no longer a sick midshipman. He had found a reason for living.

"Well then!" he exclaimed. "I will be a Hero, and, confiding in Providence, I will brave every danger."

From then on, the "Radiant Orb", as he called it, led him unswervingly to glory.

Boys planning to be officers joined ships as midshipmen, when they were as young as ten – there are records of one so young he still needed his nappies changed. For a midshipman, the pay was bad and promotion uncertain. But it was a good way of getting an education; there was the prospect of prize money, when captured enemy ships were sold; and there were chances of fame and glory.

Midshipmen learned every inch of the rigging. They learned to steer and fight, to use the sextant and they learned the complicated mathematics of navigation, and to command men. Once they had been at sea for a few years, they could take the Lieutenant's examination. After that, brave deeds or important friends would bring them to the attention of the Admiralty, who might give them promotion.

And finally, if success attended their efforts, they would be promoted Captain, and command a ship of the line, a battleship powerful enough to take its place in a great sea fight.

Chapter 2

1780

The Mosquito Shore is where Central America runs into the sea. At the mouth of the San Juan river, in a blue lagoon inside a white sandbar, the frigate *Hinchinbrooke* floated at anchor. Her captain, Horatio Nelson, was not on board.

A hundred miles up the San Juan, the air was hot and wet. The river ran brown and sinuous among marshy islands. At the desk in his tent, young Captain Nelson batted a thin hand at the mosquitoes whining round his ears. Exhausted soldiers lolled in the jungle, their red coats blotched with sweat. A jaguar coughed in the thicket. Somewhere up the river was the Castillo de la Inmaculada Concepción, a huge castle crammed with Spaniards and bristling with their guns.

The San Juan River flows eastward out of Lake Nicaragua and into the Atlantic Ocean. The western shore of the lake is only a few miles from the Pacific Ocean – a fact which had been noticed by British politicians in their cool, mosquito-free offices in London. Whoever controlled the lake and the river, the politicians realised, would have a short-cut to the Pacific, until now reachable only by travelling all the way round Cape Horn, at the bottom of South America.

Somewhere outside Nelson's tent, a man howled in delirium. The stout politicians imagined the river deep as the Thames that ran under their windows, and that Lake Nicaragua was easy. So they had ordered an army of 2,000 men to go up the river in boats. Nelson, in command of the naval side of the expedition, had run things well. But nothing would alter the fact that the river was too shallow for boats. The soldiers had

had to wade through fever-swamps full of snakes. Many were ill. There was little chance of finding out if the lake was easy or difficult.

Particularly when the approach was guarded by the Castillo.

Next morning, the red coats straggled round a bend in the river and saw the whitewashed fort perched on its hill among little farms. The men were thirsty. All filled their water bottles from a pool of crystal-clear water. Nelson drank deeply. The Indian guide shook his head, and pointed to a fruit like a little apple, bobbing in the water.

"Manchineel," he said. "Poison apple. Spanish man put her there." Something that felt like a knife twisted in Nelson's belly. All around him, soldiers were doubling up and toppling sideways on to the ground.

"Now," said red-faced, thick-headed Colonel Polson, in command of the soldiers. "We will dig trenches."

"Sir," said Nelson, through the cramps in his stomach. "The men are sick. The rainy season is at hand.

There is no time for digging trenches. If we attack now we will take the fort by storm."

"When attacking a citadel," said Polson, looking down his nose at this tiny Captain, "trenches are dug. Major!"

A Major hobbled forward, crouched over his agonizing belly.

"Dig trenches!" said Polson.

Nelson was too weak to object. An hour later, he was raving with malaria. Next day, his men carried him down to his ship in a native canoe. The siege of the fort lasted well into the rainy season, then failed. Of the 2,000 men who had gone up the San Juan river, only a hundred survived. It had been a terrible defeat. If Polson had listened to Nelson, it would have been a victory. Nelson decided two things. One, in future he would attack first, and dig trenches afterwards. And two, in future he would follow his own sense of duty, even if it meant losing friends or disobeying orders.

***

1784-5

As soon as Nelson recovered from the Nicaraguan expedition he fell in love, several times. His first girlfriend was a beautiful sixteen-year-old from Quebec in Canada – he was in the middle of deserting his own ship to marry her when a more sensible friend dragged him back on board.

His second girlfriend was a parson's daughter he met while on a visit to France to learn French, but unfortunately for Nelson, she didn't fancy him. The third, whom he met when he was posted back to the West Indies, was a beautiful West Indian of European descent; unfortunately for Nelson, she was already married. And the fourth was another white West Indian, Fanny Nesbit. With Fanny Nesbit, things went better. But by this time, Nelson had various other things to think about.

The American War of Independence had just finished. The Americans had kicked out the British. And

Nelson, the supreme England supporter, was not at all pleased. He was still less pleased that American ships continued to trade freely with the British West Indies as if there had been no war, when they should have been paying taxes to the King. The bloated merchants of the West Indies were making plenty of money out of this now illegal trade, and they were keen to carry on trading with the Americans as if nothing had happened.

Nelson's new job was to make sure that the Americans paid the taxes they owed. One day, he was standing on the quarterdeck of his ship *Boreas*, sailing down the trade wind into the harbour of Nevis, where four ships lay at anchor.

"What flag is on those ships?" said Nelson to Lieutenant Wallis, standing at his side.

"Stars and Stripes, sir," said Wallis.

"What are they doing?"

"Landing cargo, sir."

"Take the boats. Stop them landing cargo. And bring me the captains."

Away went *Boreas*'s boats, the oarsmen grinning, the officers bolt upright in the sterns. There was distant shouting.

The boats returned. Up the ship's side came the furious American captains. And there on the quarterdeck of the British frigate stood a smallish boy in a Captain's uniform, the gold lacing turned green by salt, his lank, unpowdered hair in a sort of pigtail.

"Good day to you, gentlemen," he said, with the slightest of bows. "You are trading illegally in British waters. I have the honour to inform you that I am seizing your ships in the name of the King."

A roar of protest from the Americans.

"If you wish to argue...." said Nelson.

The Americans looked down the deck at the row of guns, crouched like black pigs at their ports. They looked at *Boreas*'s large, hard crew. They looked at each other. They scowled at Nelson, and then shuffled off, to be rowed ashore.

Next morning, an angry group of Nevis merchants

stumped aboard *Boreas*. They found Captain Nelson stark naked on deck, his servant giving him a morning bath by pouring buckets of sea water over his scrawny, whitish body.

"Sir!" gobbled the merchants. "The Americans are to take you to law, and if you come ashore, you will be arrested." They stood waiting for this frightful threat to sink in.

"Really?" said Nelson. "Another bucket, if you please. And these gentlemen will be leaving." He stared at them long and hard, unaware of his naked-ness. As far as he was concerned, the authority of the King was uniform enough.

Soon, the *Boreas* and her captain had become heartily disliked up and down the islands. But Nelson did not mind being hated in a just cause – he had done his duty, and his conscience was clear. Besides, he was busy getting married at last to the young widow Fanny Nesbit.

***

1787

Not long after his marriage, he was ordered home to England. He sent his wife and stepson back on a more comfortable merchant ship, and then himself set sail on the *Boreas*. Standing on the quarterdeck, and watching the green islands sink below the blue horizon, he realized how heartily glad he was to be leaving the West Indies, with their fevers and their irritating inhabitants – none more irritating than the mosquitoes. He was greatly looking forward to a really good English sleep, with the bedroom window open and no whirring insects.

If he had known just how long the peace and quiet was going to last, he might not have looked forward to it so much.

***

No more sun. November rain drifted out of a mud-coloured British sky. *Boreas* was cold and damp, anchored on the chill, bumpy estuary of the Thames, the coast of Kent a grey smudge on the horizon. The ship's people were surly and ill-tempered, the West Indies a little room of colour and warmth in each man's head, disease and mosquitoes already forgotten. Down the ship's side climbed *Boreas*'s crew. They packed into smaller boats with their luggage, and were rowed ashore to an uncertain future.

Most of the ship's company would go to other ships. Her officers would go to other ships too, if they were lucky. The unlucky ones, who did not get jobs, would live ashore on half-pay, heart in mouth every morning when the postman called, looking for the letter from the Admiralty that would appoint them to a new ship.

Once ashore, Nelson waited confidently for his new command. And waited. And waited some more. The letter did not arrive. He went to the Admiralty in person. He found false smiles and bad excuses. Little by little, the truth dawned on him. He had done his duty for King and Country. But the West India merchants were interested in feathering their own nests, not King and Country. He had trodden on toes and made powerful enemies. Britain was at peace. The peace-time navy needed diplomats and people who could make deals, not heroes.

So Captain and Mrs Nelson moved to his father's house in Norfolk. Naturally, his father was delighted to see his son and his family come home. But Norfolk is cold, and Fanny had been brought up in the Tropics. The poor woman spent much of the winter in bed with the blankets pulled up to her chin.

Nelson, meanwhile, was fretting. There were no castles to storm or Americans to chase, and he needed things to do. He started work on the parsonage garden, bringing water from a nearby stream into a pond he had dug in the shape of a man-of-war, on which he could float miniature ships. He started to improve the small farm that went with the parsonage. And he spent many hours on the endless beaches, walking in the distant boom of the sea, deep in thought about the tactics of naval warfare.

Next winter was even colder than the first, and

Fanny hated it. Oddly, though, the appalling weather brought Nelson's hour of glory closer. All over the Continent, rivers and wells were frozen. Hungry people had to blast turnips out of the ground with gunpowder. Babies and old people froze solid in their beds. Cattle became icy statues, and in France the people rioted for bread – riots which over the next year, 1789, became the French Revolution. Nelson kept on farming and gardening, with one ear cocked towards the news from across the Channel.

By 1792, the guillotines stood in the squares of French towns. The blades inched up and whizzed down, dripping with the blue blood of aristocrats (which was, of course, exactly the same colour as the blood of commoners). Aristocratic heads thumped into the baskets in such quantities that old women used them to count the stitches on their knitting. The people of Norfolk – and the royalist Nelson in particular – were horrified.

***

1793

The final straw came in January 1793, when the head of Louis XVI, King of France, rolled blinking away from his royal body. A roar of disgust went up from England. Revolutionary France declared war. And one morning in that same month, Nelson saw from the expression on the postman's face that the long-awaited letter had arrived. He had been appointed to the command of *HMS Agamemnon*, 64 guns. Immediately, he threw a great party in the village pub at Burnham Thorpe. Norfolk men flocked to join his crew – fishermen, labourers, and three local parson's sons, who had seen what a parson's son could achieve in His Majesty's Navy.

Fanny said goodbye, weeping not very encouraging floods. (She was turning out to be not quite as brave as Nelson had hoped she would be). On a February morning of cutting wind, Nelson and his people scrambled up the side of the *Agamemnon* – a side that seemed as high as a cliff, after the low-slung frigates he had commanded. The misery of waiting for the postman lay behind him. Nelson heard the squeal of the bosun's pipes* and felt the ship's deck lift to the first of the Channel seas. He had come home.

The time for diplomacy was over. The time for heroes was at hand.

* All starred words are explained in the glossary at the back

MASTS AND SAILS

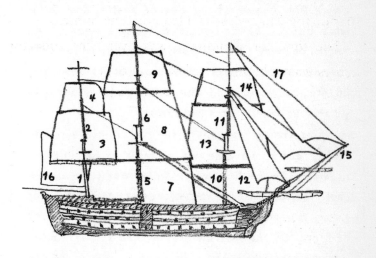

1. Mizzen mast
2. Mizzen topmast
3. Mizzen topsail
4. Mizzen topgallant
5. Main mast
6. Main topmast
7. Main sail or course
8. Main topsail
9. Main topgallant
10. Foremast
11. Foretopmast
12. Fore sail or course
13. Fore topsail
14. Fore topgallant
15. Bowsprit
16. Spanker
17. Jibs

In Nelson's day, ships went into battle in single file, known as the line of battle. One country's line of battle would put itself next to an enemy country's line of battle, and slug it out with cannons. A ship's guns pointed out of its sides. The object was to fire all one side's guns at once, in what was known as a broadside.

Ships strong enough to take their place in the line of battle were known as ships of the line.

A ship of the line was a self-propelled wooden fort. She had three masts - foremast at the bow or front, mainmast in the middle, mizzen at the back or stern. On the masts were the cross-spars called yards, from which the sails hung - courses at the bottom, topsails above courses, topgallants above topsails, royals above topgallants. At the bow was the beak-like spar known as the bowsprit.

At the bottom of the hull was the hold, full of several years' water and stores in barrels, ammunition, and gravel ballast. Above the hold was the orlop deck. Above the orlop was the gun deck, where the ship's company lived among their cannons, and the upper deck, with more cannons. At the stern* of the ship were the officers' quarters.

At the bows* were the capstan, used for hauling up the anchor, and the heads – the lavatories that hung over the rushing sea.

A ship of the line sailed best with the wind blowing from astern* or on the beam*. Naturally, she could not sail straight into the wind. Instead, she would have had to tack – to sail in zigzags – so that to make one mile towards her goal she might have to sail fifteen miles over the ground.

SHIP IN CROSS-SECTION

1. Hold
2. Orlop
3. Lower gun deck
4. Middle gun deck
5. Upper gun deck
6. Upper deck

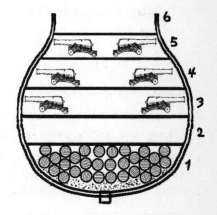

Chapter 3

1793

Beyond the rail of Nelson's ship of the line *Agamemnon* – across blue sea and behind stone quays lined with cannon – lay Toulon, chief Naval harbour of Mediterranean France. And there was Nelson on the quarterdeck, the uphill or windward side, reserved for the Captain. Ahead of him, another British ship. Astern of him, another.

The intervals between ships were exact, the manoeuvres precise. They sailed day after day in line ahead, these great British warships, watching the masts behind the sea wall, the town, the stony edge of dry, cruel France. They blockaded the port – stopped supplies getting in, and stopped the French fleet coming out to terrorise the Mediterranean. They were getting into practice for a great sea war.

The French fleet was a mess. The officers of the navy had been guillotined in the Revolution, and the ships were without discipline. For a brief moment, Toulon actually fell into British hands, before the French recaptured it. It looked like a being a long, long blockade. So the British looked around for a convenient land base, and settled on the nearby island of Corsica. There was only one disadvantage: the place was in the hands of the French.

**

1794

Nelson did not see this as a problem.

There were two principal cities, Bastia and Calvi, both heavily fortified. Nelson found himself working with the army again. But he remembered the dimwit

Polson, and the fatal delays in Nicaragua. This time he decided not to pay any attention to soldiers with smart red coats and pea-sized brains. He would use the skill and dash of the Navy, the skill and dash of men who knew instinctively how to make the best of things on the unpredictable sea.

He landed men and guns from *Agamemnon* at the foot of the mountains surrounding the city of Bastia. Experts with block and tackle, the Agamemnons hauled heavy guns to the tops of the crags towering over the town. Thus, while the soldiers were still discussing trench-digging, the sailors were pouring a terrible fire into the red roofs of Bastia below. To the astonishment of the army, the city surrendered in days.

Calvi was more difficult. Its seaward side was well defended, so Nelson decided to sneak round the back of it and attack from the land. The *Agamemnon* landed men and cannon on a beach spiky with uncharted rocks, and (with the army, who now had the decency to be impressed by what had happened at Bastia) began battering. Nelson was standing by a cannon, watching the fall of shot, when an enemy cannonball smashed into the rock beside him, blasting sand and stone-splinters into his face.

"I most fortunately escaped by only having my right eye nearly deprived of its sight," he wrote. Calvi fell. The Army took the credit for Nelson's good work. But the Navy knew who really deserved it.

***

1795

Off the coast at Toulon again, it was the old routine. Sail almost to within cannonshot of the city. Ships tack in succession, turning away until the land sinks over the horizon. Day after day, month after month...

The *Agamemnon* had now been at sea for so long that her hull was lashed together with ropes to stop her planks floating away. One day, suddenly, the flag-ship's masthead was thick with signal flags. Enemy in sight, said the signal. General chase. And there, far to the north, was the French fleet, swinging out of Toulon, heading for Corsica to blast the British bases. Closest to the British were the ships *Victoire* and the *Ça ira*.

"Carry on, Lieutenant," said Captain Nelson.

The drums thundered out the stirring rhythm of *Hearts of Oak*, the Navy's battle-tune. The sailors rolled their hammocks into hard canvas sausages and stuffed them into netting round the ship's sides, where they would protect against enemy musket bullets. The carpenters' mates ran along the gundecks with mallets, knocking out the walls of the cabins until the deck was a gleaming double line of cannons from the stern windows to the bow.

The decks were strewn with wet sand, so bare feet would not slip and dry wood would not burn. Behind wet cloth curtains in the magazine, the gunner and his mates were filling canvas bags with grainy black gunpowder.

Down in the cockpit, where the deck and walls had been painted red so the blood would not show, the surgeon was grinding his scalpels on a stone, while the surgeon's mates laid out the saws and tweezers beside the operating table and checked the leather padding on the chains that would hold down the patient.

Closer and closer came the French. High above the nets spread to catch falling wreckage, the little spidery figures of the topmen* laid out along the yards*, setting more sail. A great cheer went up from the British ships. The *Ça ira* had collided with the *Victoire*, and her topmasts* had come crashing down on deck. She lay crippled, her decks a horse's nest of spars and rope.

Crippled, but not harmless.

The *Ça ira* had 84 guns, and the *Agamemnon* was small enough to have fitted into her hold.

While two huge French ships dropped back to help the *Ça ira*, the *Agamemnon* came up behind her, swerved a little so her guns would bear, and fired a broadside into her stern windows. The cannonballs blew in the windows and screamed along the entire length of the French gundeck, skittling cannon, maiming men, splintering great oak timbers. Not one French gun could be brought to bear. Pounded to splinters, the French ship surrendered the next day.

But the majority of the French fleet got away. Nelson was not happy. His interest was in sinking *all* French ships, not just one here, one there.

"My disposition cannot bear tame or slow measures," he said. Exactly what he meant by this the world was soon to see.

***

1797

On land, the war was going extremely badly for Britain. Spain had come into the war in support of the French and Napoleon's Grand Army had now overrun the whole Continent of Europe. Orders came for the British fleet to withdraw – first from Corsica, then from the whole of the Mediterranean. Nelson had some tidying up to do, and was one of the last British ships out of the Mediterranean, not on the

Agamemnon but on the frigate *Minerve*. As the *Minerve* passed through the Straits of Gibraltar, heading into the Atlantic, the lookout hailed the deck from the masthead. "Sail ho!" he cried.

And there behind them were two mountains of sail: Spanish ships of the line, either of them capable of sinking the little frigate with a single broadside. But they were well out of range, and there was no point in panicking. So the officers sat down to dinner in the stern cabin.

Nelson tapped his ship's biscuit on the table to scare out the little insects known as weevils (they taste exceptionally bitter). The steward handed the main course of lobscouse, a dish of salt pork, soaked biscuit and lard, then a pudding called baby's leg, compounded of flour, suet and jam, boiled for several hours in a cloth. The wine went round a couple of times. Captain Nelson, Lieutenant Hardy and a Colonel Drinkwater were drinking farewell to the Mediterranean when down from the deck there floated a voice crying, "Man overboard!"

And there beyond the windows, dropping rapidly astern towards the skyscraping sails of the Spaniards, was a struggling man.

The *Minerve* lowered a boat, under the command of Nelson's great friend Lieutenant Hardy. But this boat soon fell behind, hunting for the man (who, it turned out, could not swim, and was never seen again). Meanwhile, the Spanish ships had advanced and were bearing down on the tiny boat.

"By God, I'll not lose Hardy!" cried Nelson. "Back the mizzen topsail*!" This is the sailing equivalent of jamming the brakes on. It stopped the *Minerve* more or less dead, and allowed her to drift down and rescue the boat, now within cannon-shot of the Spaniards. The Spaniards were so horrified to see the tiny frigate bearing down on them in an apparently suicidal manner that they scuttled away.

According to tradition, the drowned man's possessions were auctioned at the mainmast. Dusk closed in; a thick dusk, with a pearly look to the air. Soon the *Minerve* was in a fog so dense that it was hard to see her bowsprit from her quarterdeck. It was full of strange sounds, that fog: a creaking, and a sloshing, and the flap and bang of great sails, and from time to time a distant gun. The noises drew closer. The men on the *Minerve*'s quarterdeck became silent. They knew what it was. The gun was a signal gun. The whole Spanish fleet was right upon them.

And the little *Minerve* ran westward into the night, while the huge Spanish ships of the line wallowed past in the opposite direction, almost close enough to touch, dazzled by their own lamps.

***

By morning, the Spanish fleet was nowhere to be seen. Instead, the early sun pinkened the sails of fifteen British ships of the line under Admiral Jervis. In the far distance loomed Cape St Vincent, the bottom left hand corner of Portugal, like a rotten tooth of stone gnawing at the Atlantic swells. Nelson moved from the *Minerve* to the *Captain*, 74 guns.

The Spanish fleet would be coming north, to help protect Napoleon's troops, now threatening to storm across the Straits of Dover and into England.

The British fleet waited for them to try.

The weather was still hazy. In the milky air to the south, huge shapes appeared: great thumpers, wrote an officer in his diary, looming like Beachy Head* in a fog – pyramids of sail over death-black hulls, and in their midst the *Santîsima Trinidad*, 136 guns, the biggest ship in the world. Twenty-seven ships in all, against Britain's fifteen.

The Spanish ships were straggling along in two loose bunches. The British, having finished a leisurely breakfast, tidied away the cups and saucers and formed the line of battle, crisp and exact after years of practice on the Toulon blockade.

The object of a sea-battle at this time was to break through a gap in the enemy's line about halfway along, and engage the back half while the front half was still trying to get back up the wind.

An officer on the *Culloden*, first in the British line,

pointed out that there was no gap.

"Let the weakest fend off*!" cried Captain Troubridge. So through the line the *Culloden* charged, firing two double-shotted broadsides into the first Spaniard she saw. The unfortunate Spaniard sagged out of the line, blood pouring from her gunports into the sea.

Nelson's ship, the *Captain*, was third from last in the British line. According to the Admiral's orders, he should have followed the ship in front, and waited for his turn to put himself next to a Spaniard and open fire. But as he stood on his quarterdeck, still out of range, hearing the thunder of the guns and watching the smoke of the broadsides roll across the water, he became aware of an awful possibility. He saw that many of the Spaniards had a chance of sliding away to the safety of Cadiz harbour – unless, that is, he disobeyed orders, and broke out of the British line, and staged an independent attack of his own.

Many officers would have hesitated. Orders were the life force of the Navy, and the penalties for disobeying them were severe. But Nelson was not one to hesitate when it was a matter of his duty to his King and Country. The way he saw it, his duty was plain.

At the risk of his life, his ship and his career, he turned out of the line and hurled the *Captain* at the Spanish line, broadsides thundering. Almost immediately he was engaged with five Spanish ships. He rammed the *Captain* into the *San Nicolas*, which in the confusion had become tangled with another Spanish ship, the *San Josef*. Cannonballs screamed over the deck. The man at the wheel was suddenly an awful red fog. The wheel itself was blown to splinters. The topmast groaned wearily and fell into the sea.

"Boarders!" cried Nelson.

And off they went, the Captain's men, howling for blood, pikes and cutlasses aloft, through the bitter smoke and the thunderous noise. Nelson skipped along the *Captain*'s bowsprit, bashed his way through the *San Nicolas*'s stern-cabin windows, and fought his way on to the quarterdeck. The *San Nicolas*'s flag came down, as token of surrender.

"On!" roared Nelson, pointing with his sword at the mighty *San Josef*, hopelessly tangled alongside. Roaring death and vengeance, the Captains hurled themselves aboard the *San Josef*. And minutes later the large Spanish captain was on his knees in front of tiny powder-stained Nelson, offering up his sword in surrender. So many swords were handed over, in fact, that Nelson called over William Fearney, his barge-man, who tucked them under his arm one by one like a teacher collecting exercise books.

It was a great victory, an explosion of light in a dark time for England. Nelson was the most popular man in the fleet and the country. The wretched *San Nicolas* became known as "Nelson's Patent Bridge for boarding First-Rates." He was promoted to Rear-Admiral, and made a Knight of the Bath. Everyone (except his wife Fanny, who as usual wrote begging him not to take any more risks) was delighted with Nelson – nobody more so than Nelson himself.

He was a real hero now. And this was only the beginning.

To fire your cannon: Open your gunport. Haul on your tackles so the gun rolls back into the ship. Take your canvas gunpowder cartridge from its tight-fitting leather case, and push it down the barrel with the rammer.

Select a cannon ball, the rounder the more accurate, and ram that on top of the powder charge. For close range work, another shot - even two - may be used. On top of the shot, ram in your wad. Haul on your tackles to run out your gun. Run a copper needle down your touchhole to pierce the powder cartridge. Prime your touchhole with loose powder. Aim your gun, up and down with your quoin or wedge, sideways with your handspike.

Standing beside not behind your gun, touch your priming with your slow-match. The gun then fires with a stunning bang, and jumps eight foot back in its tackles.

Sponge out your gun with a wet sheepskin, to make sure there are no burning bits left in the barrel. The powder monkey will be waiting with the new cartridge. Repeat operation till victory is achieved.

Chapter 4

After triumph, disaster.

Darkness. Nelson standing in the stern of a rowing boat full of men. The glint of weapons. Ahead of the boat the lights of Santa Cruz de Tenerife, coming and going over the glossy backs of the Atlantic swells. In daylight, this was a town of pink and green and yellow houses above a black beach of volcanic sand, and a harbour with treasure ships. Tonight, it was a wasp's nest waiting for someone to tread in it.

From the thick darkness of the shore came little red flashes. The air was full of things that zipped and hummed. This was the second try at a small-boat landing to capture the town. The Spaniards were ready.

The British boats were close enough to the shore to hear the waves breaking on the rocks. The stone-work of the quay loomed against the stars. There was a clatter of firing from the land, and the bullets fell thick as sleet. But Admiral Nelson was there, jumping on to the quay with a hoarse cry. Nothing could go wrong.

From the inland end of the quay came a great blast of cannon-fire. The air was alive with little iron balls. A horrible smacking noise, and there was the Admiral down, falling back into the boat, the blood squirting from the wreck of his right arm.

They rowed him back to the ship. He ran up the side, arm flopping, and called for the surgeons to cut it off. He was taken below, into the dim yellow light of the lanterns, and strapped down tight to four sea chests pushed together. Naturally, there were no anaesthetics. The surgeon sliced away the mangled flesh, and sawed slowly and carefully through the living bone. Next they sewed flaps of muscle over its end to make a neat stump.

The agony was frightful, the knives cold as death. The surgeon's mate gave Nelson a dose of opium, and he was carried, shocked and silver-pale, back to his cabin. Before he fell into a pain-racked stupor, he gave orders that in future the blades of the surgeon's instruments be warmed before amputations.

When he awoke, there was a worse agony in his mind than the wound and the operation. What use would the world have for a right-handed admiral with only his left hand remaining?

***

The British fleet sailed from the disaster of Santa Cruz, back towards the disaster of mainland Europe, where Napoleon was now in total control. The spies said that in the south of France, a colossal armament was being assembled – troops, horses, carts, ammunition, supplies, astronomers, mathematicians, naturalists, and a huge number of transport ships, crammed into the harbour at Toulon. An invasion force, undoubtedly. But where was it bound?

**

1798

Once again, Nelson found himself sailing to and fro off the stony shores of France, watching the forest of masts behind the quays of Toulon for any sign of movement.

Soon, there was plenty – not from the harbour, but from the sky. After a pale sunset the wind got up from the north. It was a fresh breeze at first. Then suddenly, with a shriek and a roar, a sort of hurricane smashed into his ship, the *Vanguard*. The ship went sideways-on to the waves, rolling horribly. One by one her masts broke. There were rocks not far away, white water leaping and booming in the night. But another ship sent a line on board and towed her, half-full of water, away from the rocks and all the way to Sardinia.

Here the exhausted ship's company started work on repairs. And here, sitting in the ship's great cabin with the racket of hammering and sawing all around him, Nelson received dreadful news.

The gale that had blown the masts out of the *Vanguard* had blown Napoleon out of Toulon harbour. Three hundred ships carrying 30,000 troops, escorted by thirteen ships of the line and several frigates, had come out of harbour, slid past Nelson in the dark, and vanished into the vastness of the Mediterranean. Meanwhile, Nelson's frigates, the eyes and ears of the fleet, had been blown as far as Gibraltar. The enemy had got away. They could be anywhere.

He stood gazing at the dazzle of the sun on the sea – a small, thin figure, the eye damaged at Calvi skinned over with a cloudy film, the empty sleeve of his coat pinned to his chest. He thought of the smallness of man, and the hugeness of oceans. And a speck of white caught his eye.

It was the topsail of a ship – the brig* *Mutine*,

commanded by his old friend Hardy, now a Captain. It was good to see Hardy, and the news he brought warmed Nelson's blood. Close on the heels of the *Mutine* were ten more ships of the line, commanded by more of the old friends known as the "Band of Brothers".

That was reassuring. But the problem remained. Where were the French heading, and how in this great sea could Nelson find them? They had been seen heading southeast. Perhaps they meant to invade Sicily. Perhaps they planned to strike at Constantinople, the heart of Turkish power. Or perhaps they were heading for Egypt, a stepping-stone to the rich British possessions in India.

There was no way of being sure. On the crowded *Vanguard*, Nelson felt horribly alone. In London, his enemies would be saying that he had let the French pass under his nose without firing a shot. Where could Napoleon be?

Doggedly he settled to the hunt.

On the 4th of July, a Tunisian cruiser had seen the

French off Sicily, heading east. But on 20th July, a Genoese brig reported having seen them heading back to Sicily.

Was Napoleon planning an attack on Sicily? Surely not. Not with mathematicians, naturalists, astronomers. That sounded as if he meant to study a great and ancient civilisation.

Like Egypt.

Nelson gave the order to steer southeast. Within the week, the low land of Egypt rose from the sea, palms blowing by the dirty beaches and the minarets of Alexandria. But there were no French ships.

Desperate now, he returned to Sicily. No French there either. Nelson hated indecision. Desperate, he called in on the southern fingers of Greece. And there in a little village on the 28th of July, he met people who said (still shuddering at the narrowness of their escape) that they had seen the French, hundreds of them, sailing for Alexandria, in Egypt.

So keen had been the British pursuit that Nelson had overtaken the French in the night, got to

Alexandria before them, and left too soon.

Once again Nelson turned southeast, arriving off Alexandria on the first of August. This time, the harbour was a forest of masts. Not warship masts, though; these were troop-ships. Nelson had not slept, and he was too nervous to eat. Where were the warships? He carried on down the coast, heading for Aboukir Point, a long, low finger of land pointing out to sea at the western end of the delta of the River Nile. The sea was brown with mud brought by the huge river from the far interior of Africa.

A lookout on the top of the mast of a neighbouring British ship trained his telescope on Aboukir Point. Beyond the point he saw a line of crosses, thin and spidery with distance. Then he realised they were not crosses, but the masts and yards of fifteen ships of the line. He slid the 200 feet down a rope to the deck and made his report. The signal flags went up: *Enemy in sight*.

The French were anchored in Aboukir Bay. They lay in line of battle, the line pointing into the wind, not far from the shore, with shallow water protecting their port or left-hand sides. Nelson's great fear now was that having seen the British, they would pull up their anchors and flee. But the hours went by, and they did not put to sea. Probably they had men ashore. Perhaps they were expecting the British to spend time getting ready for battle.

Nelson's navy was always ready for battle.

The drums beat *Clear for action*. Down came the partitions on the gundecks. Up came the powder. On surged the British line, tearing down the wind towards the fight that later became known as the Battle of the Nile.

At four o'clock, with the French ships close, Nelson ordered the signal *Prepare to anchor by the stern**. The French, he realised, were relying on the British ships' fear of getting stuck in the shallow water between their line and the shore. At half past five, Nelson made the signal *Form line of battle as most convenient*. The British bore down. At the last moment, Foley in the *Goliath*, who had got hold of a

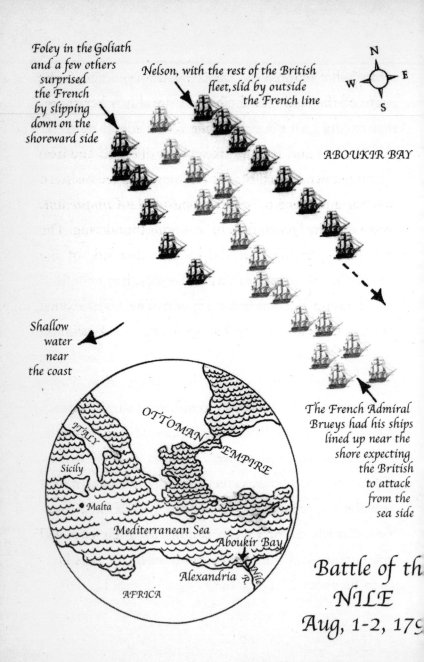

Foley in the Goliath and a few others surprised the French by slipping down on the shoreward side

Nelson, with the rest of the British fleet, slid by outside the French line

ABOUKIR BAY

Shallow water near the coast

The French Admiral Brueys had his ships lined up near the shore expecting the British to attack from the sea side

OTTOMAN EMPIRE

ITALY

Sicily

• Malta

Mediterranean Sea

Aboukir Bay

Alexandria

AFRICA

Battle of th NILE
Aug, 1-2, 179

chart* that marked the sandbanks, turned across the nose of the lead French ship, to run down her shore-ward side, giving her a raking broadside as he went. She lurched and settled, broken bits of wood and iron raining down from aloft. Then Foley dropped his stern anchor and came to a halt alongside *Le Conquérant*, second in the French line, his cannons thundering. The rest of the British fleet slid by on either side of the French line, looking for targets further down.

The sun fell towards the horizon. The desert turned the colour of blood. The battering began, and went on all night.

It was the kind of battle Nelson had always planned – his ships within pistol shot of the enemy, broadside poured on broadside, the winner being the ship with the steadiest crew and the fastest gunners. The French were brave men and brilliant seamen. But for every broadside the French fired, the British fired two. British seamen were famous for their coolness under fire. And they were commanded by Nelson, a man they loved.

This far south there is little twilight. Night came like a black blanket dropped over the battle. Each ship was a miniature hell of fire and din: the red flicker of broadsides, the dreadful screams rolling across the water, cut off short. The British ship *Bellerophon*, 74 (always known among the sailors as the 'Billy Ruffian'), had landed up opposite the huge *L'Orient*, whose cannon had almost immediately knocked her masts down. Nelson, fighting it out with two separate ships, was wounded by a shot that cut his head open, concussed him, and so shocked his secretary that the poor man could no longer write down orders.

The moon came out. In its light came another light, more terrible. "Sir!" cried a voice whose owner Nelson could not see. "*L'Orient* is on fire!"

And there it was – a little orange flicker that ran quickly down the French flagship's side, turning yellow when it found oil jars and paint tins, hungry for timber, spreading, unstoppable.

On a wooden ship, stuffed with tar and gunpowder, fire is the most terrifying of enemies. That night, it gave the British something to aim at.

A torrent of iron poured into *L'Orient*. On the deck, the French Admiral Brueys had both his legs shot off. Undaunted, he had himself stuffed into a tub of bran, in which he stood wedged upright, directing the fight until another shot cut him clean in half.

L'Orient started burning at nine o'clock. By half past, the fire was ferocious, and British ships nearby started hauling up their anchors to get away from the rain of sparks falling from the sky. The flames crept nearer the French ship's magazine. And finally, "At ten o'clock," wrote a Lieutenant Webley in the *Zealous*, "*L'Orient* blew in the air!"

She went up with a bang that silenced the guns and rattled windows in Alexandria fifteen miles away. The flash illuminated hundreds of men struggling in the crimson water. There was a rain of burning debris. Then the dark swept back and the firing started again.

By now, the ships' crews were so tired that they were falling asleep at their guns. French and British ships alike were riddled with shot. Many had lost masts, and their decks were a treacherous net of rope. Exhausted men strove at the pumps while carpenters patched holes between wind and water. But on they fought, battering away. In the end only two French ships, the *Guillaume Tell* and the *Généreux*, managed to escape. In Nelson's mind, there was no point in fighting sea battles unless the enemy was utterly destroyed.

The sun rose on a bay paved over with wreckage and corpses. Clouds of flies drifted out from the land. Nelson, his bandaged head aching horribly, surveyed the carnage.

"Victory," he said, "is not a name strong enough for such a scene."

He had a point. The British were once more in control of the Mediterranean. Napoleon and his army were marooned in Egypt. And the Nelson touch – swift action, iron discipline, total destruction – had shown its worth.

Someone pulled *L'Orient*'s mainmast out of the water, and made from part of it a coffin which he presented to Nelson. Nelson was delighted with this thoughtful gift. He put British crews onto the six captured French ships, and the whole fleet sailed to Naples.

It was difficult to find enough men to volunteer for the hard, dangerous life of the Navy. The shortage was made up by groups of sailors known as press gangs, whose job it was to rove the country near seaports, kidnapping likely men and dragging them on board against their will.

These unhappy fishermen and farmhands and shopkeepers, snatched away from wives and children, were usually ready to revolt against their officers.

To make sure this did not happen, ships of the Navy were run according to a ferocious set of rules called the Articles of War.

Under the Articles, many offences carried the death penalty. Small offenders - drunkards, perhaps - would be made Lord of the Heads, whose job was to clean the lavatories - a filthy job on a ship carrying up to eight hundred men.

More serious crimes were punished by flogging. The guilty man's shirt was stripped off, and his hands tied to a handy piece of rigging. The bosun's mates brought out the velvet bag with the cat o' nine tails, a whip with nine lashes decorated with elegant but painful knotwork.

The criminal received the number of strokes pre-scribed by the Captain. His mates would then take him away and slosh on vinegar and brown paper to heal his lacerated back.

Executions, on the surprisingly rare occasions they were carried out, took the form of hangings from the yardarm*.

Chapter 5

A few days later, the fleet dropped anchor under the volcano in the blue, blue bay of Naples. It seemed to Nelson like a warm, bright Paradise. He had just won the greatest sea victory of the war, and he was ready for some relaxation. Also, he was recovering from a bang on the head with a cannon-ball; so perhaps he was not thinking very clearly.

At that time Naples was part of the Kingdom of the Two Sicilies. It was ruled by cousins of the French royal family, which had been murdered during the French Revolution only five years earlier. As far as the King and Queen of Naples were concerned,

Napoleon was a friend and supporter of the people who had killed their relations. Naturally, they saw him as their deadly enemy. They and their kingdom were now allied with Britain, which felt the same way.

So the King and Queen were delighted to welcome Nelson, the Hero of the Nile. They had charming palaces scattered over the slopes of Vesuvius, the volcano that towers over Naples. Here the King, who was cruel and stupid, occupied his time with massacres of wild animals that he called hunting. And the Queen, who was cruel and clever, occupied her time with seventeen children and many lovers.

There was an important British couple there, too, – the British Ambassador Sir William Hamilton, the King of England's man in Naples, who occupied his time with his world-famous collecton of ancient vases and statues; and his wife Emma, Lady Hamilton, who occupied her time with Nelson.

Emma Hamilton was exceedingly beautiful, with dark eyes so vast and expressive that it was easy not to notice that she was becoming stout. In her youth in

England she had been far from respectable. She had been the mistress of several rich men, and was famous for her marvellous "Attitudes", in which she dressed up as famous people from history and myth for the benefit of large and fashionable audiences.

Though slightly more respectable since her marriage to Sir Willam, she had not lost her love of showing off. She greeted the Hero dressed *alla Nelson* – in a blue dress encrusted with large gold anchors. At a party she gave for Nelson, she decorated a statue of the tiny, one-eyed, one-armed Hero with a crown of laurel leaves and real diamonds, and the band played *See the Conquering Hero Comes*.

Many British heroes would have thought this a bit over the top. But Nelson, so cunning at sea, was an innocent ashore. The King of Naples made him Duke of Bronte. Nelson lapped it up, delighted, as the child of a Norfolk parson, to be getting all the attention, and to be with such a beautiful woman. While his wife Fanny sent him letters about pots of jam and other boring domestic matters, Emma, who had known a lot more men in her life than Fanny had, continually told him how marvellous he was, and took him to parties. As far as Nelson was concerned, this was exactly what he deserved.

***

1799

But real life was about to burst in on Paradise. Napoleon's armies were on the point of conquering Naples. So Nelson's new friends, the King and Queen, got him to transport them and their treasure to Sicily.

With the King gone, his enemies immediately rebelled and seized Naples. This disgusted Nelson, the great royalist. He returned to Naples, anchored his ships in line of battle with gunports open and facing the city, and demanded that it once again submit to the rule of the King and Queen, who were on board.

It had been some time since the shot had glanced off his head at the Nile, but perhaps his brains were still a bit scrambled. Since his long-ago vision of the

Radiant Orb, he had had an exaggerated respect for Kings and Queens. Even so, it is astonishing that he did not realise exactly how vicious and useless the King and Queen of Naples really were. But he did not. He did exactly what they asked him to do.

He hanged Admiral Caracciolo, for example – a rebel, but a good and noble man – from the yard-arm of his own ship, cutting the rope so the corpse dropped into the harbour without decent burial. And he turned a blind eye to the scenes of horror by the gallows in the main square, where scores of men and women were hanged, with a man swinging from the victim's legs while a dwarf jumped up and down on the shoulders.

After the suppression of the revolution, Nelson hung around in Naples, apparently hypnotised by Lady Hamilton. Orders came from England instructing him to leave. He ignored them. Certainly he went cruising, and sank the *Généreux* and the *Guillaume Tell*, the only two French ships that had survived the Battle of the Nile. But it was as if he was on another planet. While Napoleon left his army to rot in Egypt and returned to France to think again about invading England, Nelson stayed in Naples, drinking wine, playing cards, and listening to Emma telling him what a splendid fellow he was.

But in England, people were getting annoyed. His wife was tired of getting long letters from him explaining exactly how much he liked Lady Hamilton. And the Navy wanted to know what was so important that it was stopping him obeying orders. Finally, he was ordered to return to England, and told that as punishment for his slacking, he would not be allowed to return on a ship of the line. There was a time when this would have mattered hugely to Nelson; not now. He set off instead on a grand trip across Europe, accompanied by Lady Hamilton and Lady Hamilton's husband.

The party, consisting of fourteen coaches and three large baggage vans, created a great stir wherever it went. Away from the sea, Nelson did not look impressive. "He is covered with stars, ribbons and medals, more like a Prince of the Opera than the Conqueror of the Nile," said one aristocratic gossip. But all the way across Europe the common people turned out in their thousands to cheer him. They brought their children to be touched by him. They gaped in at the windows while he dined. They applauded him when he went to the theatre. Encouraged by Lady Hamilton, Nelson lapped it up.

Even bigger and noisier crowds were waiting in England.

But so was trouble.

Things started well enough. In Ipswich the mob took the horses out of his carriage and dragged it through the streets themselves. The same thing happened in London. But after that, things went steeply downhill. His wife was furious that he was spending all his time with that Hamilton woman. The King, too, who liked heroes to be respectable, greeted him coldly.

Nelson found that he was no longer welcome in the houses of people who had once been his friends. To the shocked surprise of the whole of London, he told his wife he never wanted to see her again. The hero of the mob, he was shunned by his own, and he did not understand why. The life of a hero on land was excessively complicated, and made him deeply unhappy. There was only one thing he could do, and he did it. He asked for a job at sea.

**

1801

Fortunately for Nelson, the Admiralty did not mind how shockingly he behaved on land, as long as he could give the enemy a hard time at sea. He was appointed second in command of a fleet being formed for service in the Baltic. Once he was back at sea, everything once again became beautifully clear. He could forget his own difficulties and concentrate on doing his duty for King and Country. Just now, King and Country needed help badly.

The problem was this. The Russians and

Scandinavians had got tired of their ships being stopped and searched by the British, to check whether they were carrying supplies to France. So they declared Armed Neutrality. This meant that they would not allow British ships into the Baltic Sea to pick up supplies of timber, Stockholm tar, rope, and other gear vital to the running of a wooden sailing navy.

The traditional British answer to this kind of declaration was to send in the fleet, and get a new treaty signed. If the treaty was not agreed, the fleet would open fire. Following this principle, the British government decided to send a fleet to negotiate with the Russians and Scandinavians.

The Commander of this negotiating fleet was to be the diplomatic but unwarlike Admiral Sir Hyde Parker, with Nelson as his undiplomatic but warlike second in command in case things got violent.

Sir Hyde was a stout, greedy mariner of 61, who had recently managed to marry an eighteen-year-old girl. For days the fleet waited at anchor in the North

Sea off Yarmouth while the newlyweds made plans for a Grand Ball (much to the amusement of the sailormen, among whom the bride became known, on account of her extreme podginess, as the "Batter Pudding"). But then Nelson arrived, in a hurry to get going. And he soon made sure that the Ball was cancelled.

The fleet sailed for the Baltic. The Batter Pudding was most upset, and her frightful old husband in a great sulk. Both blamed Nelson, which worried the one-armed second-in-command a good deal. He knew how important it was to get on with his commanding officer. He decided to try and make amends.

As the fleet crossed the Dogger Bank, an officer mentioned that he had once caught a turbot, most delicious of fish, on exactly this spot.

"Catch another!" cried Nelson. A turbot was duly caught. Nelson sent the fish across to Sir Hyde, who ate it and pronounced it excellent. From then on, he and Nelson were the best of friends.

The Kattegat is the narrow stretch of water between Sweden and Denmark, and the highway for ships entering the Baltic. Its narrowest part, the Sound, was guarded by the great fort of Cronenburg. As the British fleet went down the Sound, the fort opened fire (and missed). It looked as if the time for talking was over, and the time for fighting was at hand. The place to fight was Copenhagen, Denmark's capital.

The city lay on the edge of the Sound, guarded by anchored battleships, floating batteries* bristling with cannon, and strong forts. There were two channels – the King's Channel running past the city, and the Outer Deep, parallel to the King's Channel on the far side of the big sandbank known as the Middle Ground.

The north wind would take the British ships down the Outer Deep. They would anchor at the bottom of the Middle Ground, wait for the wind to change, then sail up the King's Channel, anchor opposite the

Danish line, sink the ships and wreck the forts. Sir Hyde Parker would wait to the north of the sandbank, in reserve.

It was a typical Nelson plan, depending entirely on a complete shift in the wind, without which the fleet would be trapped and disaster certain. Someone asked what would happen if the wind did not change. Nelson replied airily that it would. The Danes had taken away the navigation buoys that marked the channel, so Nelson sent out men in little rowing boats in the dark, to sound the depths and put down buoys of their own.

On April 1, the wind blew from the north – exactly what was required by the British to take them down the Outer Deep. The Danes on the quays of Copenhagen watched nervously as a mountain-range of white canvas glided down the Deep, out of range of their guns.

All that night anxious Danes poured across from the city, transporting ammunition to the ships and batteries. As often before a battle, Nelson slept badly.

When he stuck his nose out on to the quarterdeck of his ship next morning, he saw the wind was now blowing from the south, as he had hoped. Up came the anchors. Down sailed the British – down the grey King's Channel, cleared for action, gunports open, heading for the spires of wonderful Copenhagen.

The Danes were good seamen and tough people – made tougher by the fact they were defending their capital city. Each British ship anchored opposite a Danish ship and opened fire. The two sides were evenly matched. Because of the shallows there was no chance of getting inside the Danish line, as at the Nile. The British rate of fire was faster than the Danish. But every time a Danish crew was wounded or tired, a rowing boat would bring fresh men out from the shore. The two lines hammered away at each other with an awful doggedness.

On the approach to battle, Nelson had been as jumpy as a cat on hot bricks. Now his flagship, the *Elephant*, was hammering broadsides into the Danish flagship. As cannonballs howled past his ears, he became calm and sunny. Lieutenant Langford shouted above the racket, "Admiral Parker flying no 39, my lord."

Nelson nodded. Number 39 was the signal to break off action. He put his telescope to his blind eye. "I really do not see the signal," he said. And the ships fought on.

This was typical Nelson behaviour. But this time, he was not ignoring orders. It seems probable that Sir Hyde Parker, perhaps remembering the turbot, was flying the Recall flag to give Nelson an excuse for honourable withdrawal if the action was too hot for him.

Nothing was too hot for Nelson. And if it was not too hot for Nelson, it was not too hot for his men.

Late in the day the Danish flagship, wrecked and burning, went sagging off down the tide. A cease-fire* was agreed. The cease-fire became an armistice*. The British ships sailed off up the Baltic, and hung threateningly off the Russian port of Reval (now Talinn, in Estonia) with their gun-ports open. Not, Nelson hastened to point out to the sweating Russians, that he was threatening anyone. It was simply that he wished to salute the new Tsar.

No more was heard of Armed Neutrality.

Every night, the seamen hung up their hammocks, jammed into the gundeck like sardines. Every day they lowered hanging tables between the guns and sat down to dinner. Instead of bread there was biscuit, square, inch-thick, hard as iron and creeping with weevils. For meat there was salt pork or beef, soaked in fresh water, then boiled. For vegetables, there were dried peas. The fat that rose to the surface of the boiling meat was called slush, and was used to grease the rigging.

This diet, though revolting, was better than a lot of men got at home. There were few complaints - though there were riots when a doctor tried to introduce porridge instead of bread and cheese for breakfast. Besides, there was plenty to drink. There was lime juice, full of vitamin C to keep scurvy at bay. There was a gallon of beer a day. And there was rum, issued daily. The men could be relied on to drink as much rum as they could get hold of at all times.

Chapter 6

London meant stardom. London meant riot, and frenzy, and being mobbed in the street. London meant reading that he was a hero in the newspapers, while trying not to notice the insulting cartoons of himself and Emma Hamilton. London meant living in a house Emma had decorated with pictures of Nelson and Nelson's battles and Nelson's clothes and telescope and hat, navy blue everywhere, shoals of gold anchors.

London meant excitement, vanity, making political speeches that got him into trouble. Again, London was a madness he found it hard to understand.

1803-1804

Then in 1803 he was appointed commander-in-chief, Mediterranean Fleet, and hoisted his flag on the *Victory*, and left London far behind.

The Long Watch began.

The *Victory* was 226 feet long and weighed 3000 tons. Her sides were of English oak, two feet thick. She was stout as a castle. She carried 850 men and 100 guns. Slow but deadly, she slid down to the Mediterranean, and took up the watch on Toulon – this time at a distance, hoping the French fleet could be lured out, so they could be once and for all destroyed.

Life on the *Victory* was calm and regular, intensely soothing after the riot of London. Every day Nelson was called at six, with a weather report and a statement of the ship's course*. He breakfasted with his staff, his chaplain and his doctor on tea, hot rolls, toast and tongue.

From seven to two he worked. The ship's band then provided music until a quarter to three, when the drummer played the *Roast Beef of Old England* as a signal for dinner. For the officers, there were three courses, followed by fruit, with three kinds of wine. Nelson ate little – a spot of chicken, perhaps, with macaroni – and (in an age where men consumed wine like water) drank less.

After coffee, the Admiral's staff walked on deck for an hour. Then it was time for tea and conversation until eight, when cake and rum punch arrived. The Admiral was in bed by nine.

Day after day, month after month, this routine continued. The French did not venture out of Toulon. The French admiral died of a heart attack, apparently brought on by too much walking up the hill to see if the British were still on the horizon.

Napoleon's armies were ready to invade England. There were 150,000 men in the Channel ports, and Napoleon himself had been sighted in Boulogne, glowering greedily at the white cliffs of Dover. All that was needed was for the French fleet to come out of the harbours where it was lurking, and shepherd the invasion barges across the Channel to strike their deadly blow.

**

1805

In January 1805, after the *Victory* had been on watch for eighteen months, she was taking on water in Sardinia when a frigate came hurtling in with shocking news. Villeneuve, the new French Admiral, had taken the fleet out of Toulon. The enemy was at sea.

Once again Nelson set off into the blue wastes of the Mediterranean, looking for the enemy, too worried to eat. Once again, all the harbours were empty. He sailed all the way to Egypt, and found no French. Then he found out that the French had come out of Toulon, been battered by a gale, and gone straight back in again.

Though all the worry had been in vain, it was affecting his health. His good eye, battered by bright sun and salt spray, was fading. He coughed a lot, and an old wound had flared up again. And still he waited, stomach knotted with tension, for something to happen.

In the end, happen it did.

On 30 March, Villeneuve once again brought his fleet out of Toulon. Nelson heard the news five days later, from one of his frigates. As usual, he suspected that the French would head east. Day after day he patrolled their route; no Frenchmen.

Finally, a merchant ship told him that the enemy was heading west. The British fleet fought light winds and contrary currents, trying to get through the Straits of Gibraltar.

Nelson's worry increased. Perhaps the French had gone up to the English Channel to support the invasion. Perhaps they were on their way to attack Ireland. Or had they gone across the Atlantic, to beat up the West Indies?

If Nelson guessed wrong, his career would be over, the war against Napoleon lost.

Then, finally, he had real news. The Scottish

captain of a Portuguese ship told him that the French had sailed for the Caribbean, and that they had had a whole month's start.

So on piled every stitch of sail, and down the Trade Winds surged the British fleet. But the bays of the West Indies were empty. The French had been and gone.

On 13th June Nelson started back for Europe. French rubbish floating in the sea told him the enemy was not far ahead. In July the British fleet, empty-bellied from short rations, sighted a smudge on the eastern horizon that was Cape St Vincent, the southwestern corner of Portugal. And a couple of days later, Nelson put his foot on dry land for the first time in nearly two years.

His ships were so worn out that the French had assumed they would sink. But they had all but caught Villeneuve, who had scuttled off northward, had a minor brush with another English fleet, and taken refuge in a Spanish harbour.

The final battle was at hand.

Nelson returned to England to prepare for the fight. He had been famous when he left. Now, he was capable of bringing London to a complete halt.

Pompous courtiers and stuffy politicians did not understand it. This little man was loved like a brother by everyone in England, from beggars to Dukes. He had made terrible mistakes, been truly horrible to his wife, and set up house with that ghastly Emma Hamilton. He was vain, toothless, one-armed and one-eyed. But when the light of his kindness shone upon you, it was impossible not to love him.

He helped ordinary seamen down on their luck. The Duke of Wellington, Britain's greatest general and a future Prime Minister, had at first thought him a big-headed fool. But when he got a clear sight of Nelson's genius, he thought him the greatest man in England.

At the house in Surrey he shared with Emma, the great Admiral played with their five-year-old daughter Horatia, and walked by the garden pond he had christened the Nile. And he worked in his study, per-

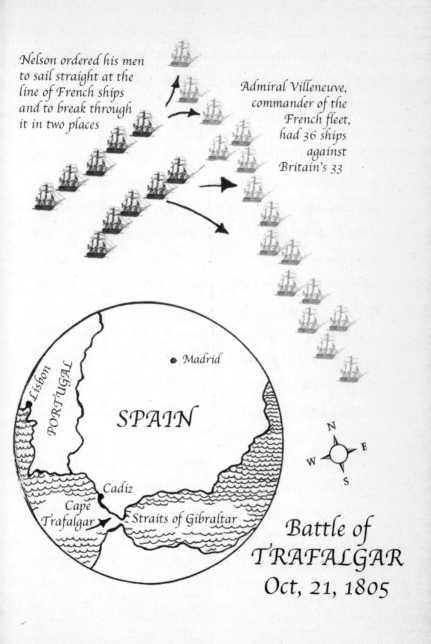

Nelson ordered his men to sail straight at the line of French ships and to break through it in two places

Admiral Villeneuve, commander of the French fleet, had 36 ships against Britain's 33

Lisbon
PORTUGAL
SPAIN
• Madrid
Cadiz
Cape Trafalgar
Straits of Gibraltar

N
W E
S

Battle of
TRAFALGAR
Oct, 21, 1805

fecting the battle-tactics he called the Nelson Touch, that would save Britain from Napoleon.

On 2nd September 1805, a fast carriage skidded to a halt outside the front door. A lieutenant jumped down, and gave him the news. Villeneuve and the French were in Cadiz, and had linked up with the Spanish fleet. The hour had come.

Nelson said goodbye to Emma and Horatia, who were horribly upset. Then he went down to the *Victory*. The great ship moved steadily out into the Channel, south and west, across the Bay of Biscay, down the coast of Portugal to Cadiz and the nearby cape of Trafalgar, the last headland on the left before the Straits of Gibraltar.

Cadiz was a great port, but there were more than 30 French ships of the line in the harbour, and no port could keep that many ships fed and supplied for ever. Sooner or later, the fleet would have to come out.

Nelson would be waiting.

He and the *Victory* hovered over the horizon from Cadiz. In the great cabin, he gathered his captains and explained the Nelson Touch.

He would bring the British fleet down on the enemy line in two files, and break the line in two places. It was extremely dangerous – the ships at the front of the files would be sitting ducks for the enemy cannons for a long time before they would be in a position to return fire. But it would mean that dozens of enemy ships could be engaged at once. It would, said Nelson, the light of war glinting in his single eye, "bring forward a pell-mell battle, which is what I want."

On the 20th of October, the enemy finally came out of Cadiz – 36 sail of the line against the British 33. All that night, Nelson shadowed them. At dawn the next day, they were nine miles to the east, silhouetted against the dawn across an oily sea ruffled with cat's paws of breeze. A bloody dawn: red in the morning, sailor take warning.

Nelson put on his second-best coat, the chest covered with the stars of his orders and decorations. A lieutenant pleaded with him to wear something less showy – the French had sharpshooters in the rigging, with instructions to shoot anyone in officer's uniform. Nelson shrugged him off. "I shall now amuse the fleet," he said. "Pascoe!"

"Sir," said Lieutenant Pascoe, in charge of hoisting the signal flags*.

"Make, *England confides that every man shall do his duty*."

Pascoe hesitated. "*Confides* is seven flags, my lord. Could we make it *Expects*?" ("Expects" is a word that can be signalled with one flag, and there was a lot of signalling to be done that morning.)

"Make it so, Mr Pascoe."

Up went the flags.

"What else does he think we're going to do?" growled Captain Collingwood, in the van of the other line.

The *Victory* bore down on the enemy line at a snail-like one and a half knots – less than two mph. The French were firing ranging shots. The first fell short. The next hummed high over *Victory*'s masts. With the third, a hole appeared in *Victory*'s topgallant*. There was a long swell coming in from the southwest now, and the sky had a thick, pasty look.

On the gundecks, the gunners tied their black handkerchiefs tight round their ears to blunt the awful detonations to come. One man polished his gun. Another danced a hornpipe. It was all very tidy and cheerful, with an edge of madness.

The French found the range.

The air was suddenly full of hurtling iron. Nelson's secretary was cut in half. The maintopmast came down with a groan and a crash. The French ship ahead – the *Bucentaure*, Villeneuve's flagship – was close enough for Nelson to see the heads of the men on deck, the gunners sponging out their cannon inside the gunports. The side of the French ship slid past the *Victory*'s bowsprit, big as a block of flats. Then the *Victory* was sailing past the lines of gleaming glass windows in the Frenchman's stern.

"Fire," said Admiral Lord Nelson.

Into those windows fired each of the *Victory*'s guns, double shotted, in a long, rippling broadside that smashed twenty French guns off their carriages and mangled 400 men. Then Hardy, captain of the *Victory*, put the ship alongside the *Redoutable*. All around, British ships slid slowly into the throng, went alongside an enemy, and commenced pounding. The enemy line was a shambles. The slogging match had begun.

At a quarter past one, Admiral Nelson, who had been strolling the deck, clapped a hand to his shoulder, sank to his knees, and fell over sideways. A sniper in the *Redoutable*'s rigging had finally found his target.

"They have done for me at last," he said. He drew a handkerchief over his face and medals, so the men would not see who it was that had been wounded. Then they carried him down to the red-painted cockpit, where the surgeon was already working, up to his armpits in blood.

The bullet had broken Nelson's back, nicked an artery and entered his lung. It was a terrible wound, and Nelson was bleeding to death, beyond human help. He grew steadily weaker. Hardy reported to him that the battle was going well, fourteen enemy ships having surrendered.

Nelson said, "Take care of poor Lady Hamilton. Kiss me, Hardy." Soon after that, he said, "Thank God I have done my duty."

And there, in the hellish crash of the guns, under the yellow lamps swinging to the enormous rise of the sea, he died.

***

The Battle of Trafalgar was a famous victory. Eighteen French and Spanish ships had been captured or destroyed. One British ship was lost. The Nelson Touch had worked beautifully.

That night the swell increased still further, and a gale shrieked in from the west. It piled the sea into toppling grey hills of water. Ships already shattered by gunfire wallowed helpless, driven by wind and sea towards the sharp black teeth of the land. Men exhausted by battle found no rest. They were up for days and nights on end, plugging shot-holes, mending rigging, striving in huge seas to take their mauled comrades in tow.

Ships sank and were wrecked, and men died of sheer tiredness. Only when the wind dropped could the survivors fall into a black and bottomless sleep, and wake to the knowledge that Britain once and for all had control of the seas, and was safe again from tyrants.

But even the joy of this fact was blunted by the news, spreading through the corkscrewing ships of the fleet, that Nelson was dead.

London heard on 6th November. Strangers wept on each other's shoulders. Nelson was brought back on *Victory*'s deck, pickled in a barrel of brandy. He was buried with high ceremonial in St Paul's Cathedral, in the coffin made of *L'Orient*'s mainmast that he had been given after the Battle of the Nile. London's noblest square was named after Nelson's greatest victory, and he stands in it today, on his column, gazing over the Thames towards the Channel.

All London came to watch his funeral. All knew that Nelson more than anyone else had saved Britain from invasion by Napoleon in a war won by "far-distant, storm-beaten ships, upon which Napoleon's Grand Army never looked, but which stood for ever between it and the domination of the world."

Emma Hamilton was not invited.

KEY DATES

1758 – Born in Norfolk.

1771 – Midshipman Horatio Nelson joins HMS *Raisonnable* at Chatham.

1773 – Joins Captain Lutwidge on a trip to the North Polar seas.

1774 – Joins HMS *Seahorse* and goes off to the Indian Ocean to harass the allies of Napoleon.

1776 – Leaves the Indian Ocean after a bout of malaria and returns to Britain on board HMS Dolphin, where he has his famous vision of the "Radiant Orb".

1780 – The Nicaragua expedition and the attempt to capture the Castillo de la Inmaculada Concepción end in disaster after Colonel Polson ignores Captain Nelson's excellent advice.

1784-85 – Nelson, in command of HMS *Boreas*, teaches the newly-independent Americans a lesson when they refuse to stop trading illegally in British waters.

1787-93 – Nelson, without a ship, gets very bored and frustrated at home in Norfolk.

1789 – French Revolution begins.

1793 – Louis XVI, king of France, is guillotined. Nelson is given command of HMS *Agamemnon* and sent to war with the French revolutionary government.

1794 – Nelson gains control of Corsica which had been in the hands of the French.

1795 – The French ship *Ça Ira* is forced to surrender.

1797 – Spain sides with the French against Britain. At the battle of Cape St Vincent, Nelson takes the surrender of the Spanish ships *San Nicolas* and *San Josef*.

1798 – The Battle of the Nile.

1801 – Battle of Copenhagen: Admiral Lord Nelson of Bronte and the Nile puts a stop to armed neutrality in the Baltic.

1803 – Nelson appointed commander-in-chief of the Mediterranean Fleet.

1805 – The Battle of Trafalgar. Nelson, commanding the British fleet from HMS *Victory*, dies a hero's death.

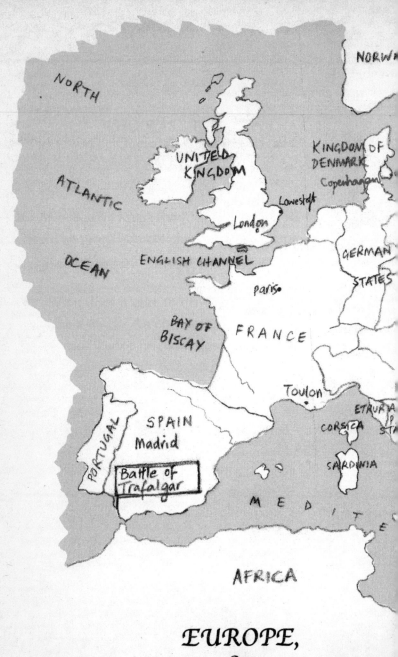

NORTH

ATLANTIC

OCEAN

NORW

UNITED
KINGDOM

KINGDOM OF
DENMARK
Copenhagen

Lowestoft

London

ENGLISH CHANNEL

GERMAN

STATES

Paris

BAY OF
BISCAY

FRANCE

Toulon

ETRURIA
P
STA

CORSICA

PORTUGAL

SPAIN

Madrid

SARDINIA

Battle of
Trafalgar

M E D I T E R

AFRICA

EUROPE,
1805

GLOSSARY
(All the starred words explained...)

armistice – agreement for a permanent end to a war

astern – behind a ship

batteries – groups of cannon, usually on shore

on the beam – at the side of a ship

Beachy Head – a famous cliff-face on the southern coast of Britain

Bosun's pipes – whistles used to give orders on ships

bow – front of a ship

brig – small, fast square-rigged ship

cease-fire – temporary interruption to fighting

chart – a map of the bottom of the sea

course – direction a ship is heading

fend off – to push another ship away in order to avoid a collision

frigate – medium-sized, fast warship, used for watching the enemy and delivering messages

mizzen (sails) – sails at the rear of a ship (see diagram on p.41)

port – left

signal flags – flags representing words or letters of the alphabet, used to signal messages from ship to ship before the invention of radio

starboard – right

stern – back of a ship

topgallant – see sail diagram on p.41

topmasts – see sail diagram on p.41

topmen – nimble sailors who leap around high in the rigging to adjust sails

topsail – see sail diagram on p.41

yardarm – the outside end of a yard (see below)

yards – long thick poles from which sails hang